Can You See?

By Keith Pruitt, Ed.S

Words of Wisdom

2018

Introduction

Pictures are lots of fun. We take a picture to help us remember what something looked like that we saw. We might take pictures on a trip. We might take pictures when our family is together. When are some times that you take pictures?

Do you have pictures at your house? Perhaps you could bring a picture of yourself to school of when you were younger. Do you have pictures of places you have visited?

Is there a favorite picture in your house?

At our house, we love to take lots of pictures. Sometimes you have to look very close to see what is to be seen. Here are some of my favorite pictures. Can you point to what the picture is asking about?

--Keith Pruitt

Can You See the Deer?

Can You See the River Boat?

Can You See the Duck?

Can You See the Nests?

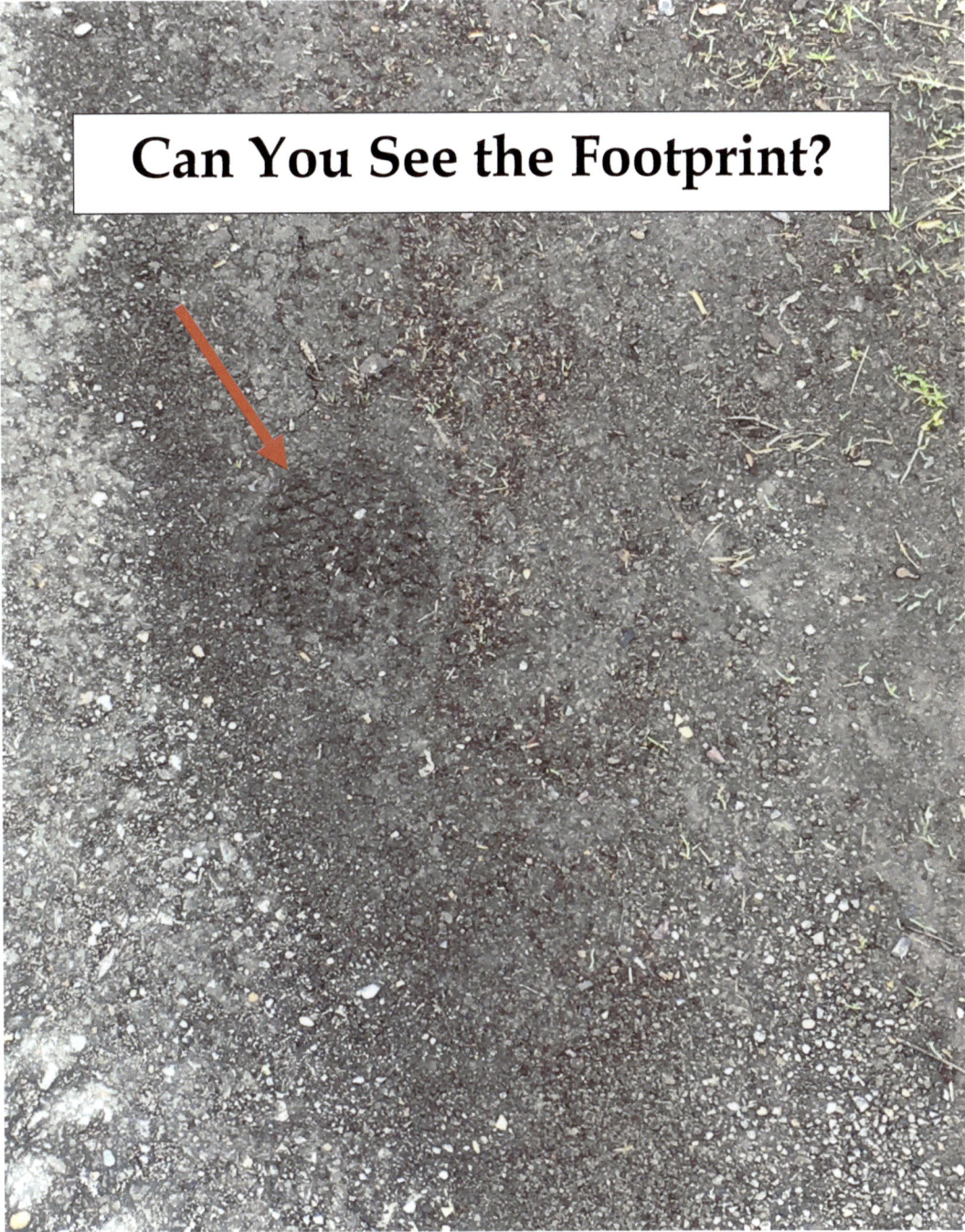

Can You See the Footprint?

Can You See the Waterfall?

Can You See the Moss?

Can You See the Snail?

Can You See the Steam?

Can You See the Reflection?

Can You See the Opossum?

Can You See the Worms?

Can You See the Creek?

Can You See the Turtles?

Can You See the Tree Fungus?

Can You See the River Rapids?

Can You See the Pine Cone?

Can You See the Giraffe Ice Sculpture?

Can You See the Food?

Can You See the Bird?

Can You See the Spinning Top?

Can You See the Rainbow?

Can You See the Sunset?

Can You See the Guitar?

Can You See the Moon?

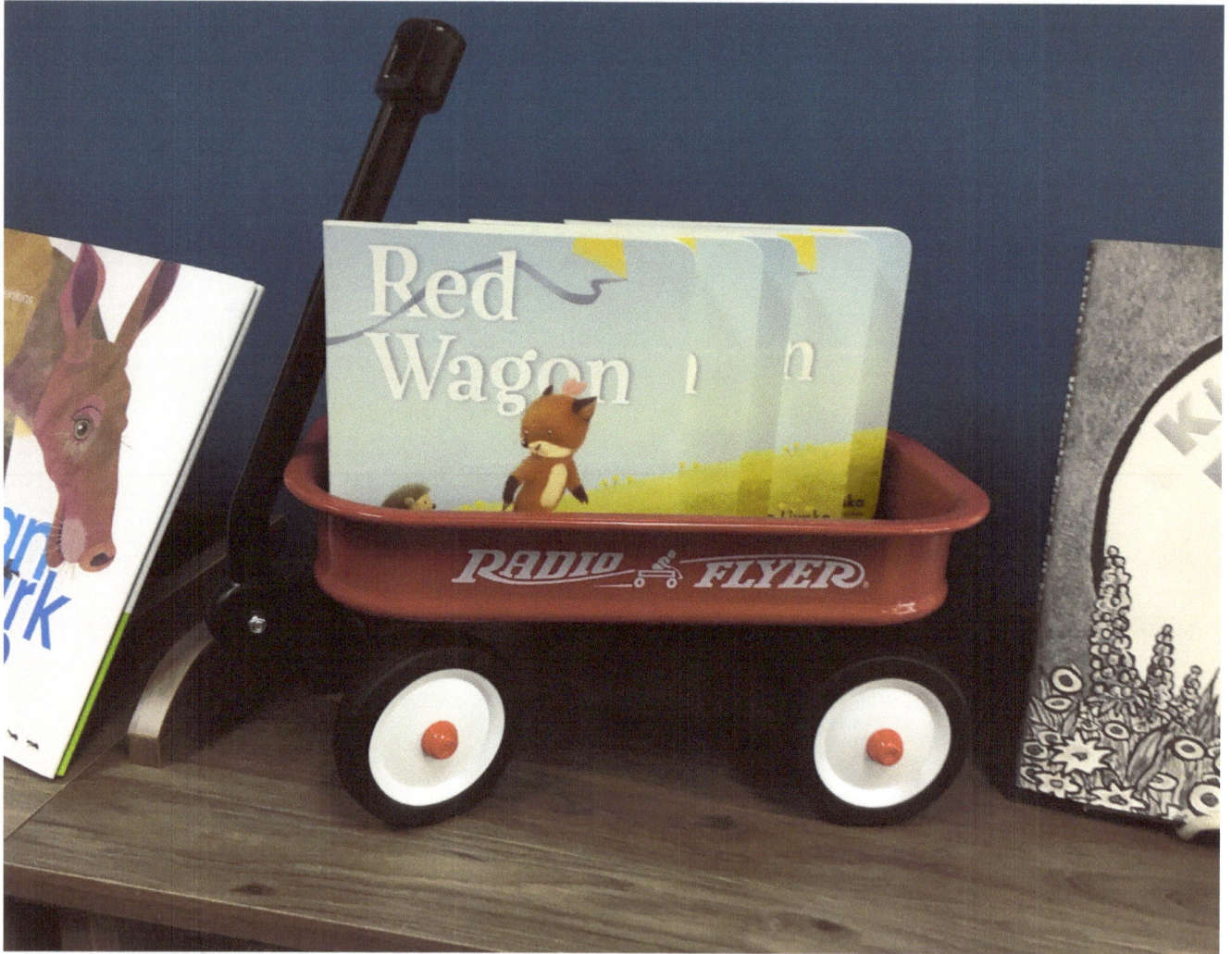

Can You See the Red Wagon?

Can You See the Squirrel?

Can You See the Groundhog?

Can You See the Barge?

Can You See the Kite?

Can You See the Helicopters?

Can You See the Capitol?

Can You See the Pigeon?

Can You See the Fountain?

Can You See the Clock?

Can You See the Clouds?

Author's Note

Thank you for allowing me to share with you some of my memories through pictures. I hope these have been of value to you. I wanted to let you know something about each picture. You see each picture was taken by me, so each comes with a story or a memory.

I live near Old Hickory Dam in Nashville, Tennessee and visit there often to walk the nature trails. The park is owned by the Army Core of Engineers and the trails are great and filled with wildlife. Because the Cumberland River forms Old Hickory Lake, river traffic and wildlife are abundant. Pictures 5, 6, 11, 14, 16, 19, 20, 21, 23, 33, and 34 were taken there.

Cedar Hill Park is one of the great parks of Nashville which has 100 plus parks. I love walking there in the summer time. The challenging and divergent trails make for a different hike each time I walk there. Pictures 7, 8, 9, 10, 12, 17, 18, and 31 were taken there.

Photos 13 and 22 were taken at my home.

My home is in the historic Old Hickory Village a community built by the DuPont family in 1918 for the workers of the DuPont gunpowder factory. They manufactured gunpowder for the military in World War I. Photos 15 and 29 were taken there.

Holidays are always important in our family tradition. Photo 23 is from Thanksgiving and 25 is from Christmas.

Photos 26 and 27 were shots taken in LaVergne, Tennessee.

The Grand Ole Opry is something that is near and dear to me. Photo 28 was taken the night that Chris Young became the newest member of the Opry. That's him on stage.

In the bookstore that we use to own, in the children's section, is where photo 30 was taken.

That fat little furry critter, as we call them, was taken as I was walking in Knoxville, Tennessee near the Pilot Headquarters.

Washington D.C. is one of my favorite places. I've been there several times and we even wrote a book about it. Pictures 35, 36, 37, and 38 were all taken in the nation's capital.

Picture 39 was taken in the Cheekwood Mansion in Nashville, Tennessee. Cheekwood is the botanical gardens in Music City.

Taking pictures from a plane can be fun. Number 40 is above the clouds over New Jersey as I was traveling to New York City.

Thank you for reading my book of pictures. Now look at all the things you can see around you.

www.ingramcontent.com/pod-product-compliance
Lightning Source LLC
Chambersburg PA
CBHW060832270326

41933CB00002B/65